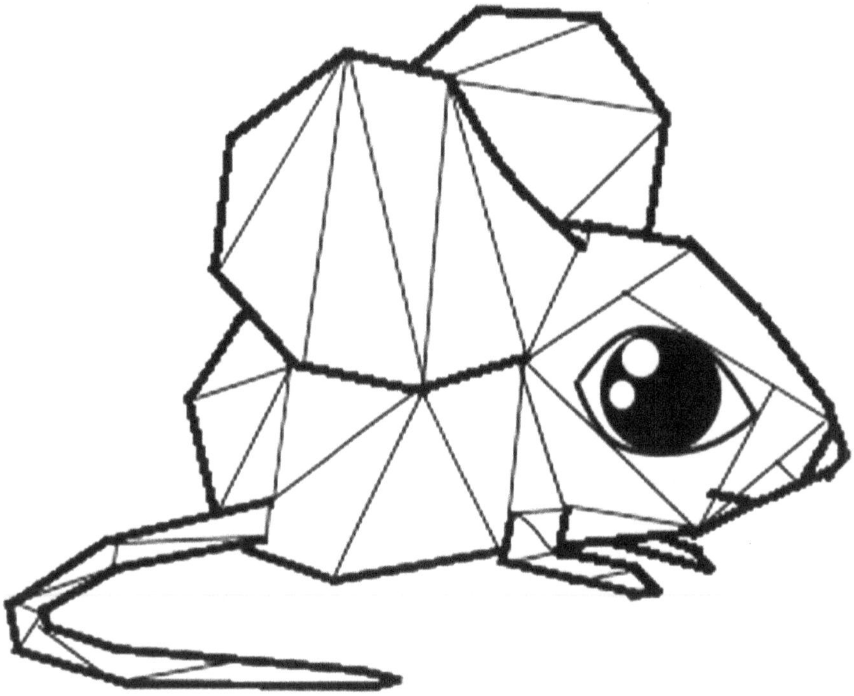

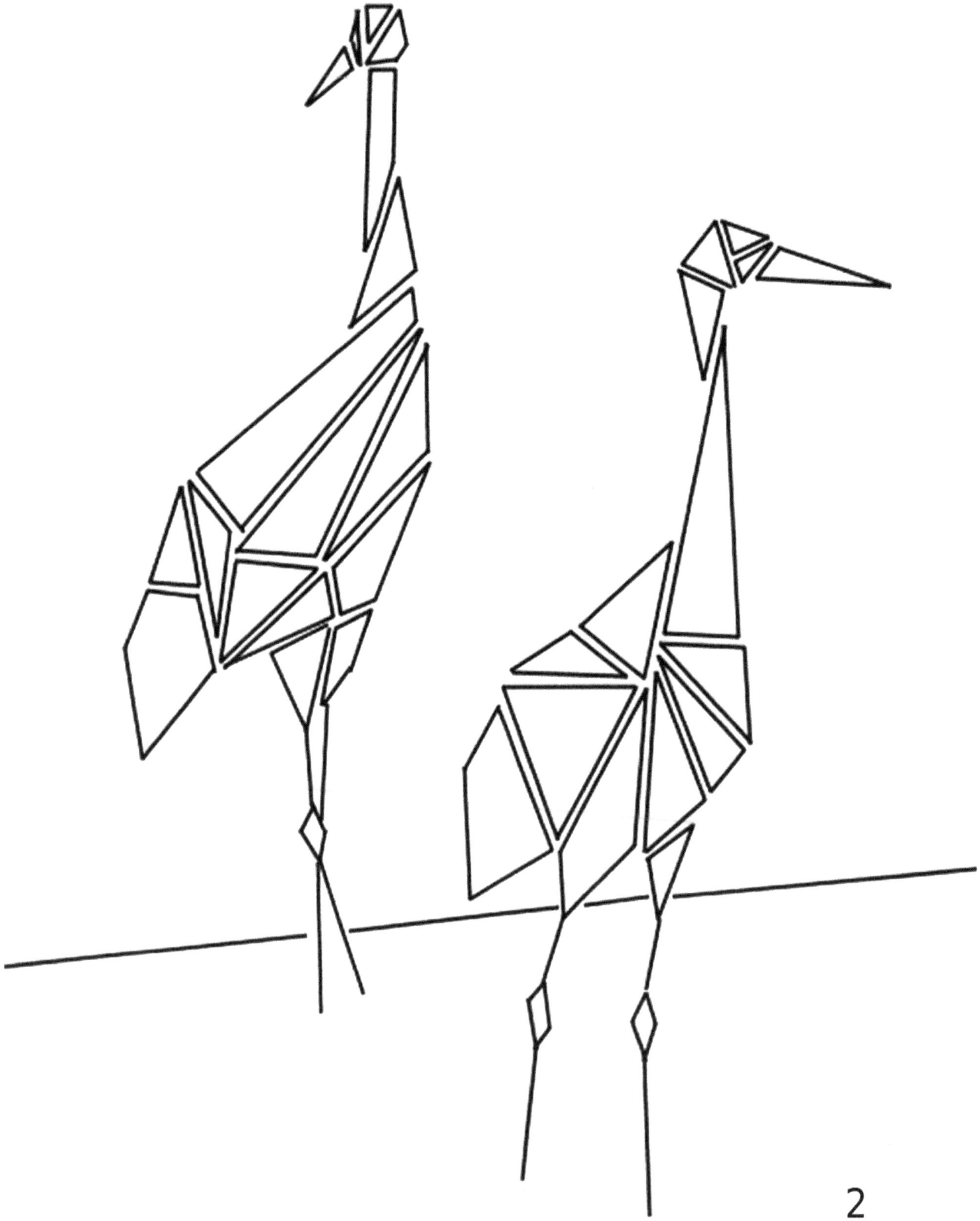

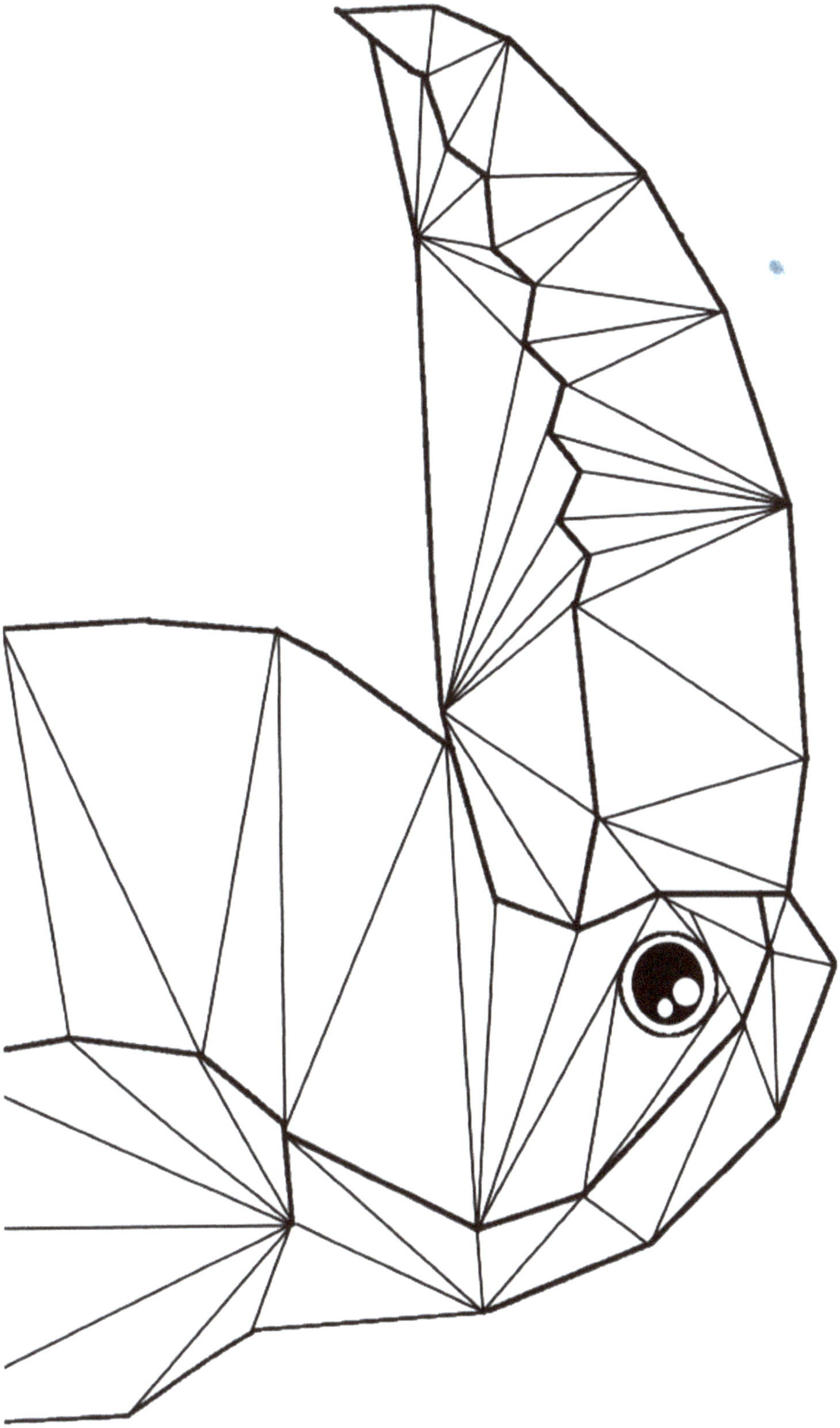

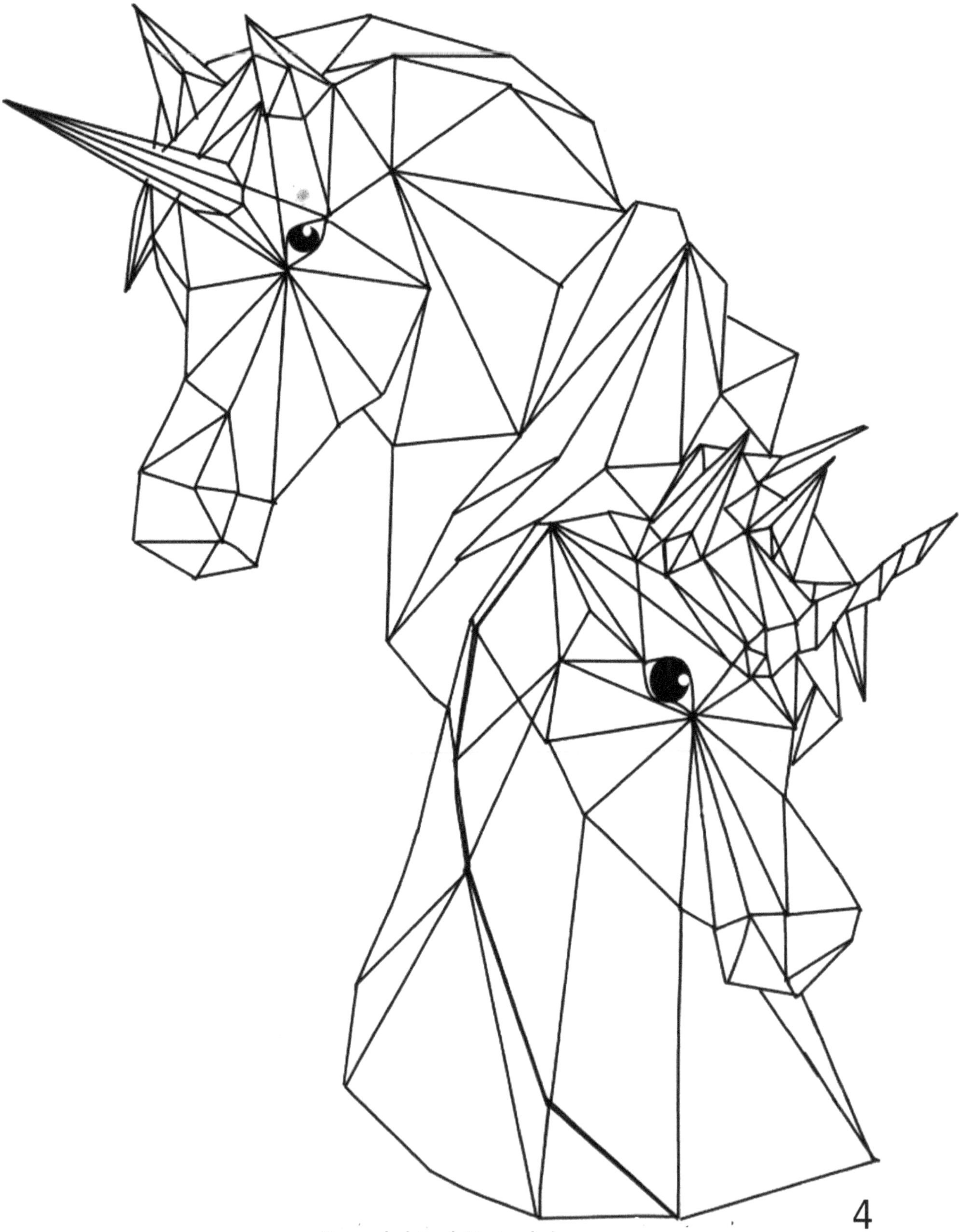

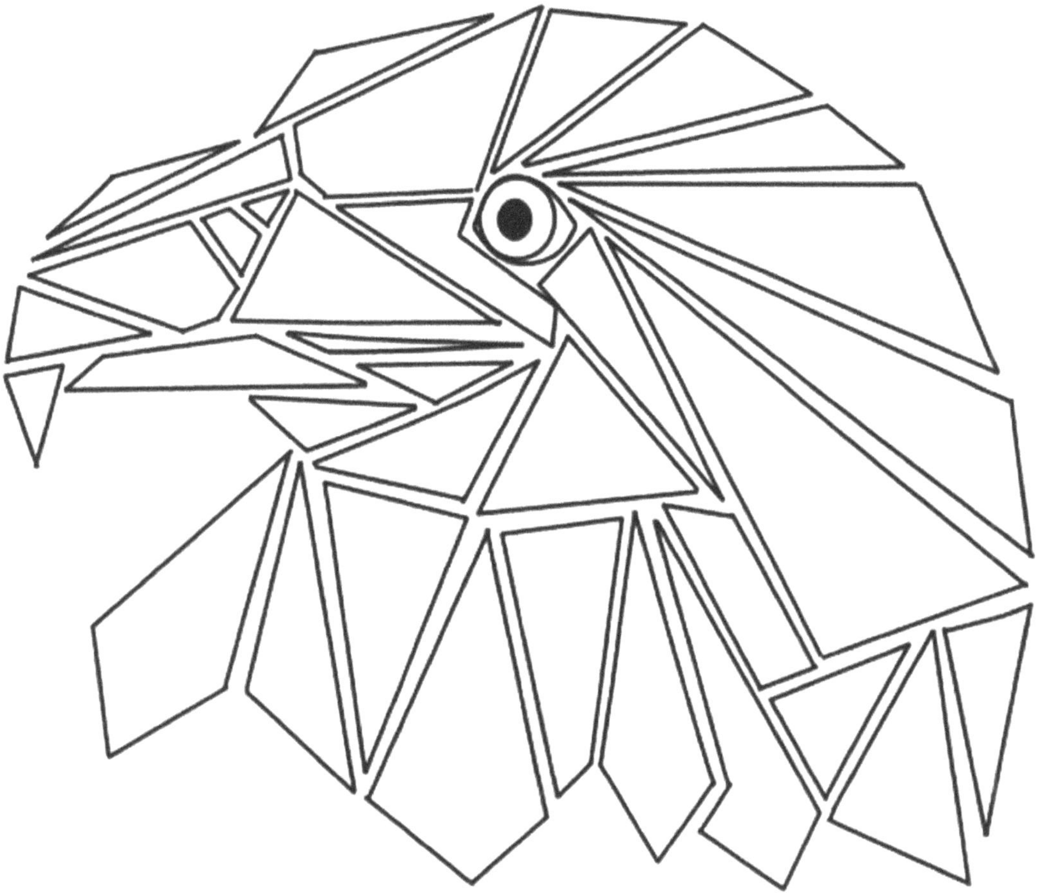

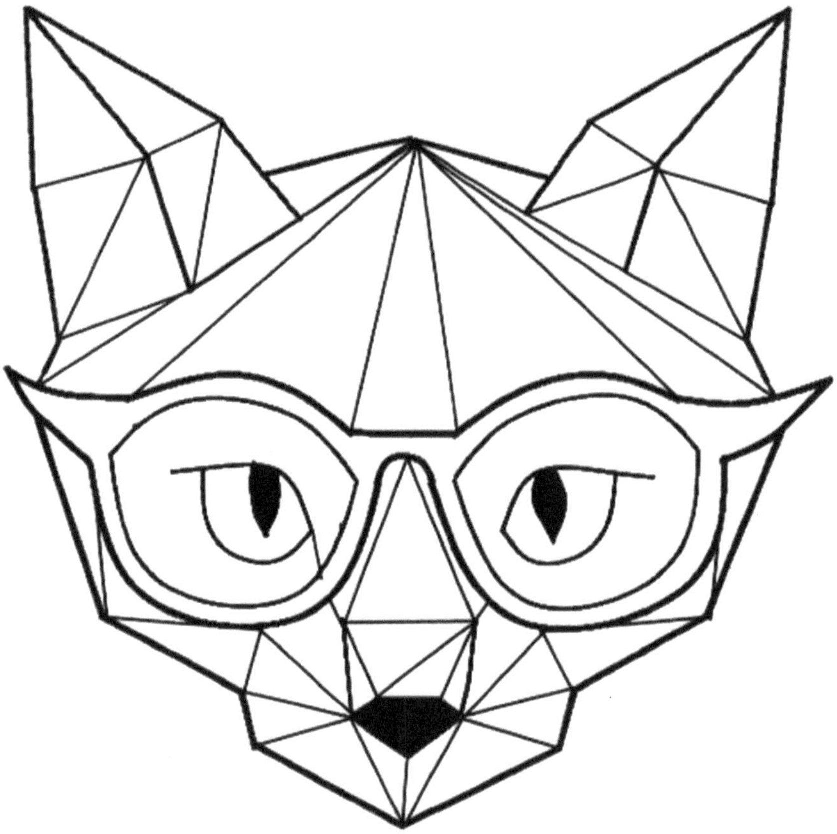

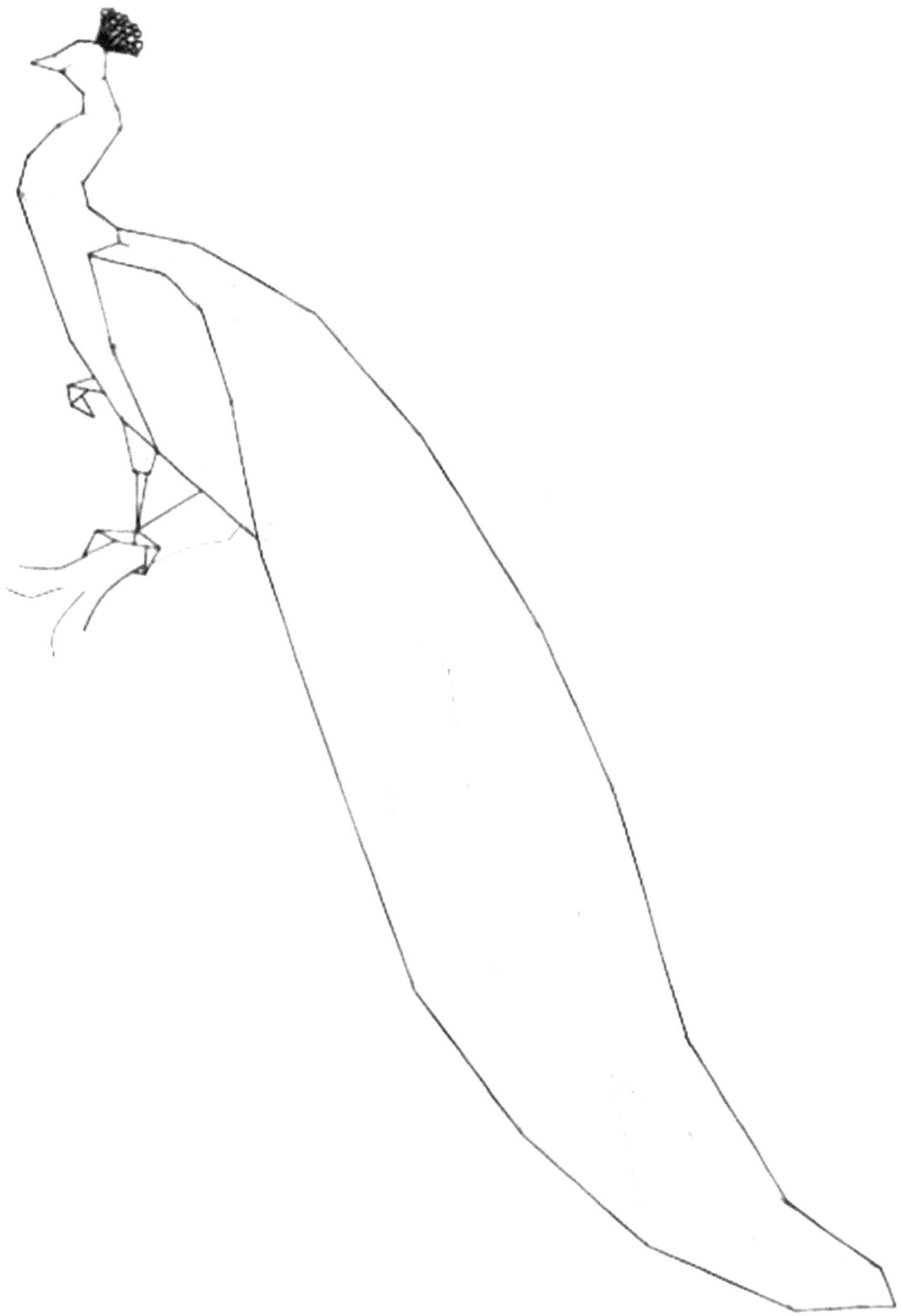

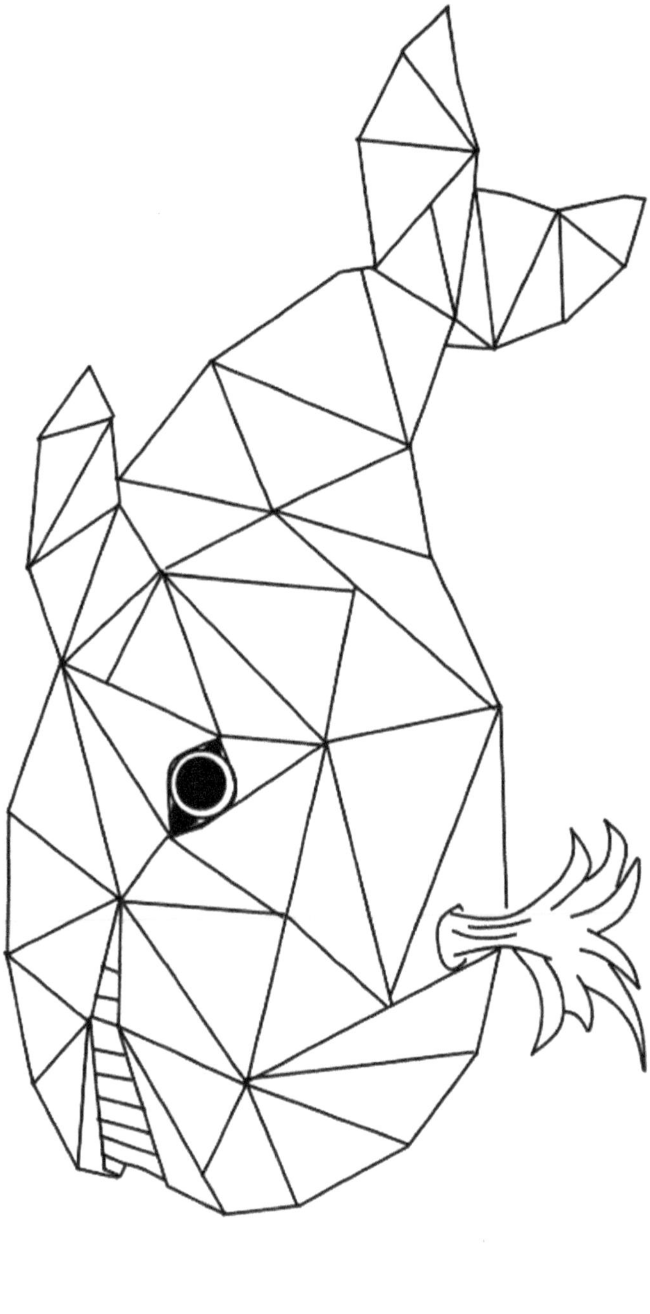

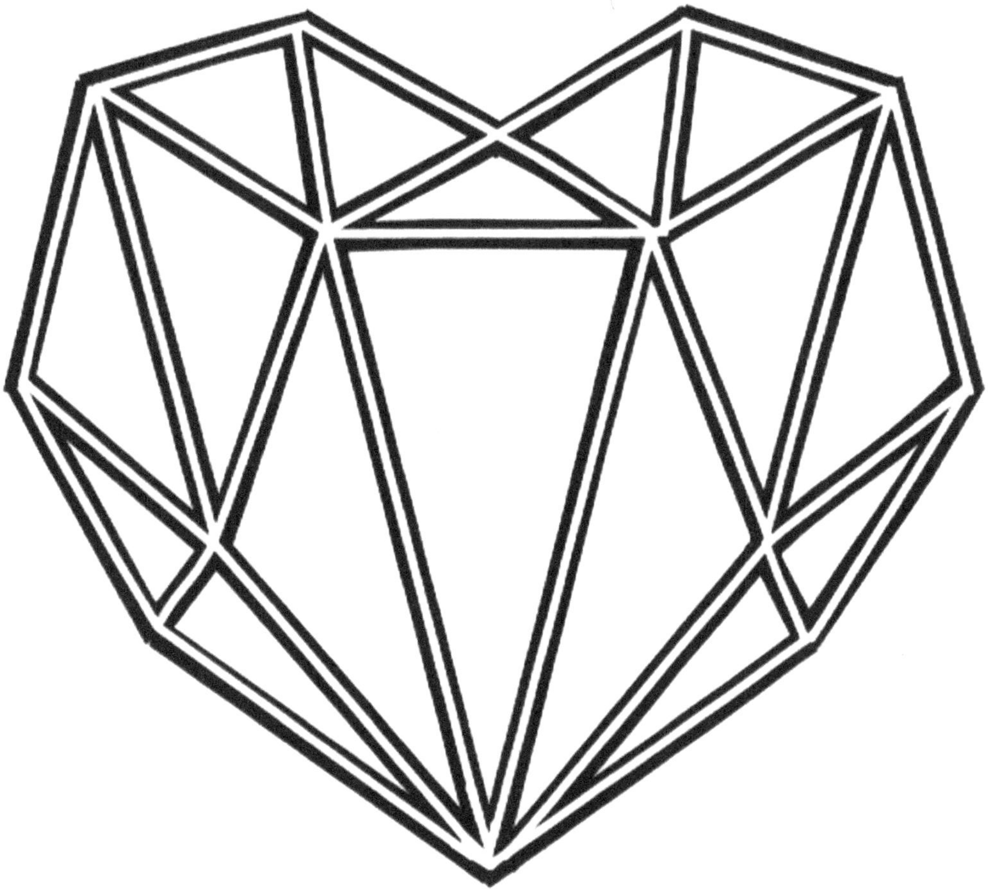

Copyrighted Material

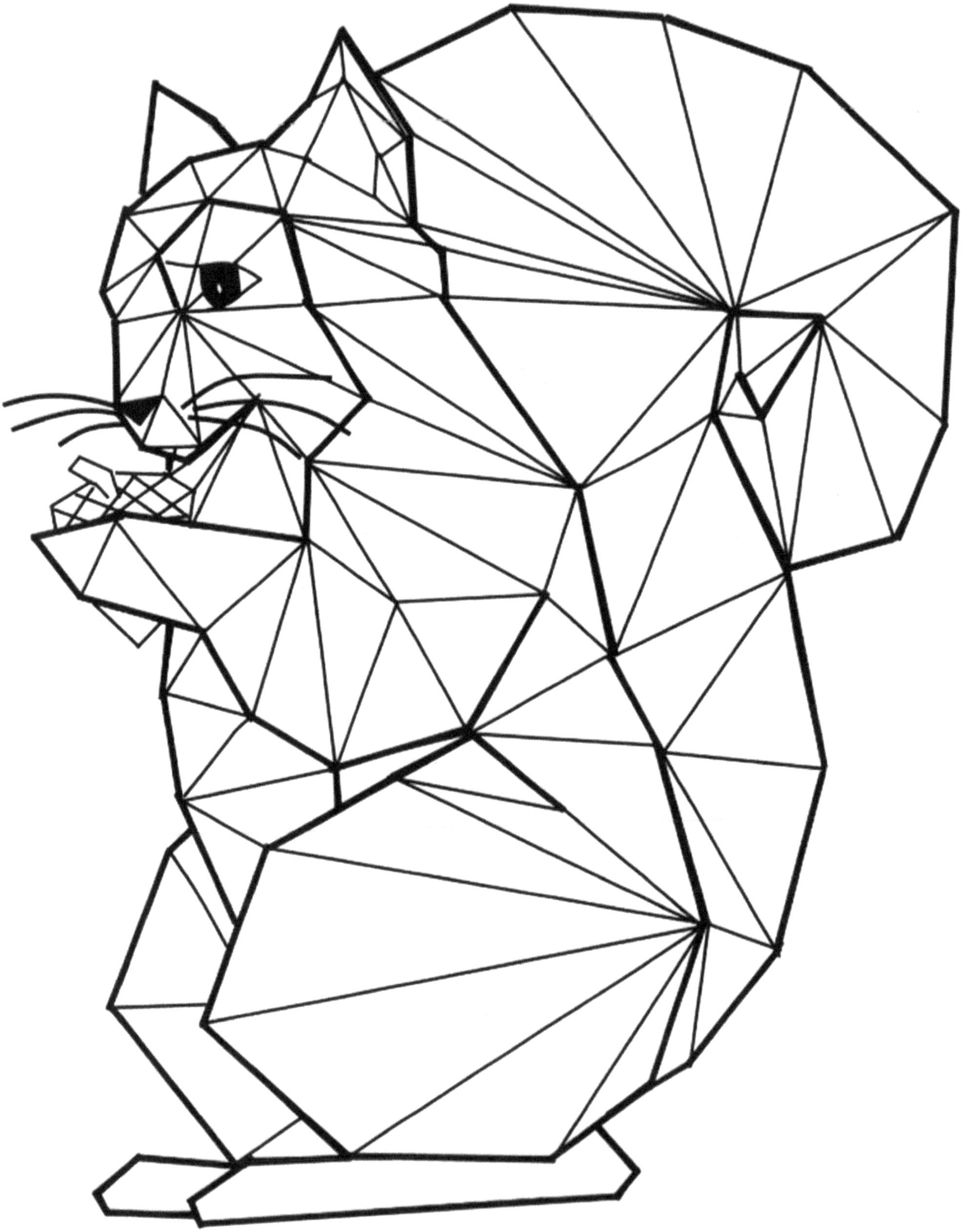

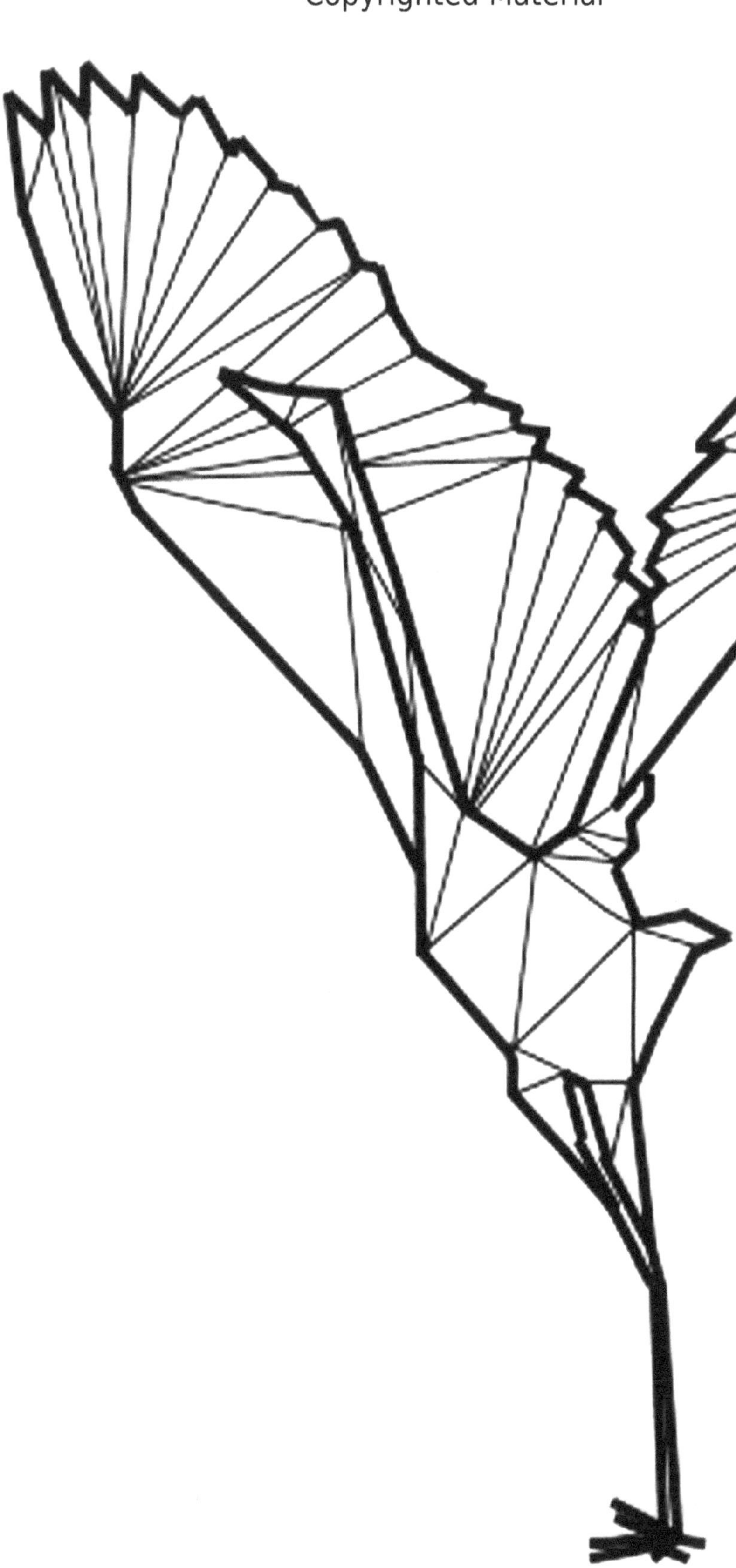

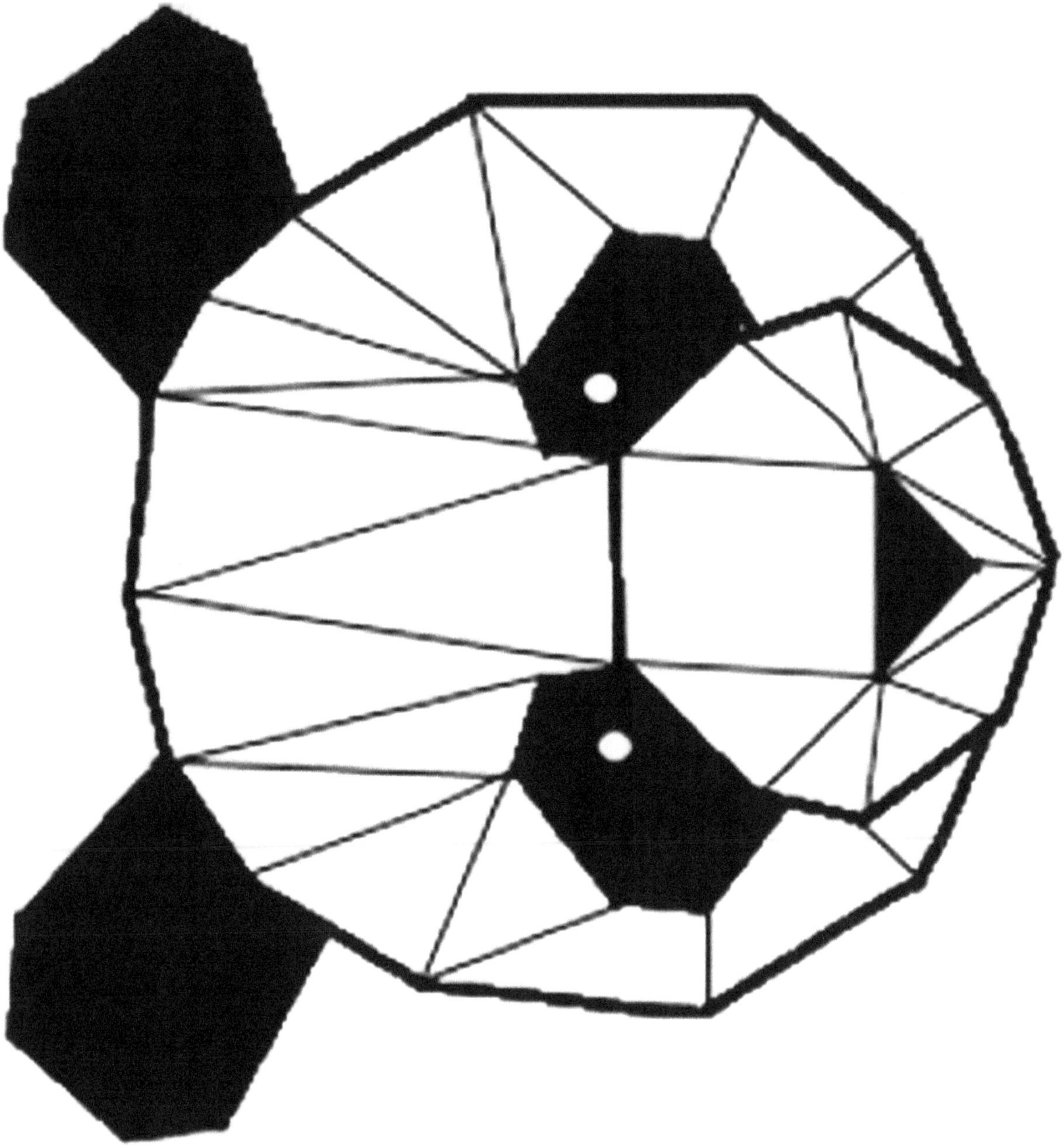

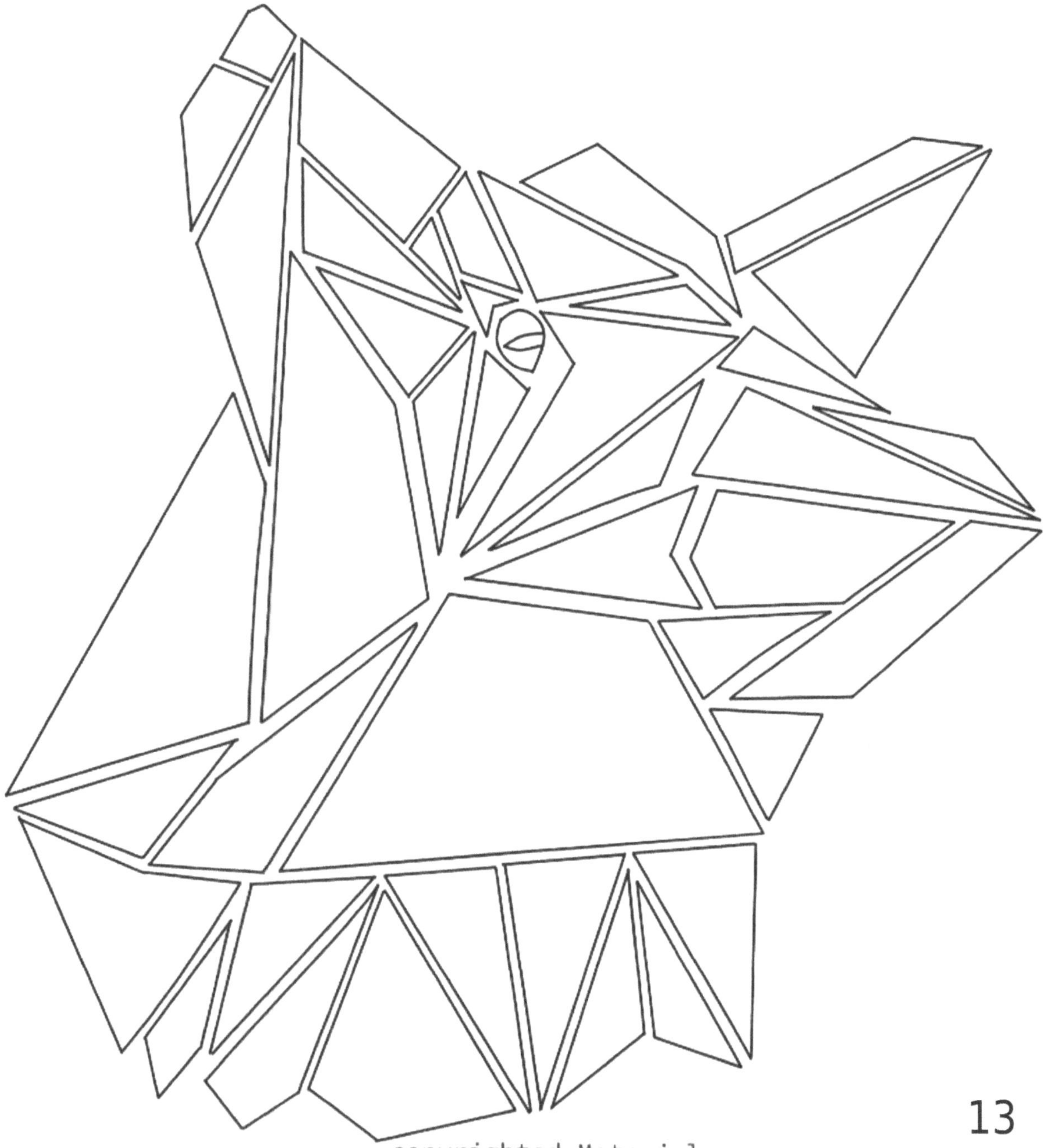

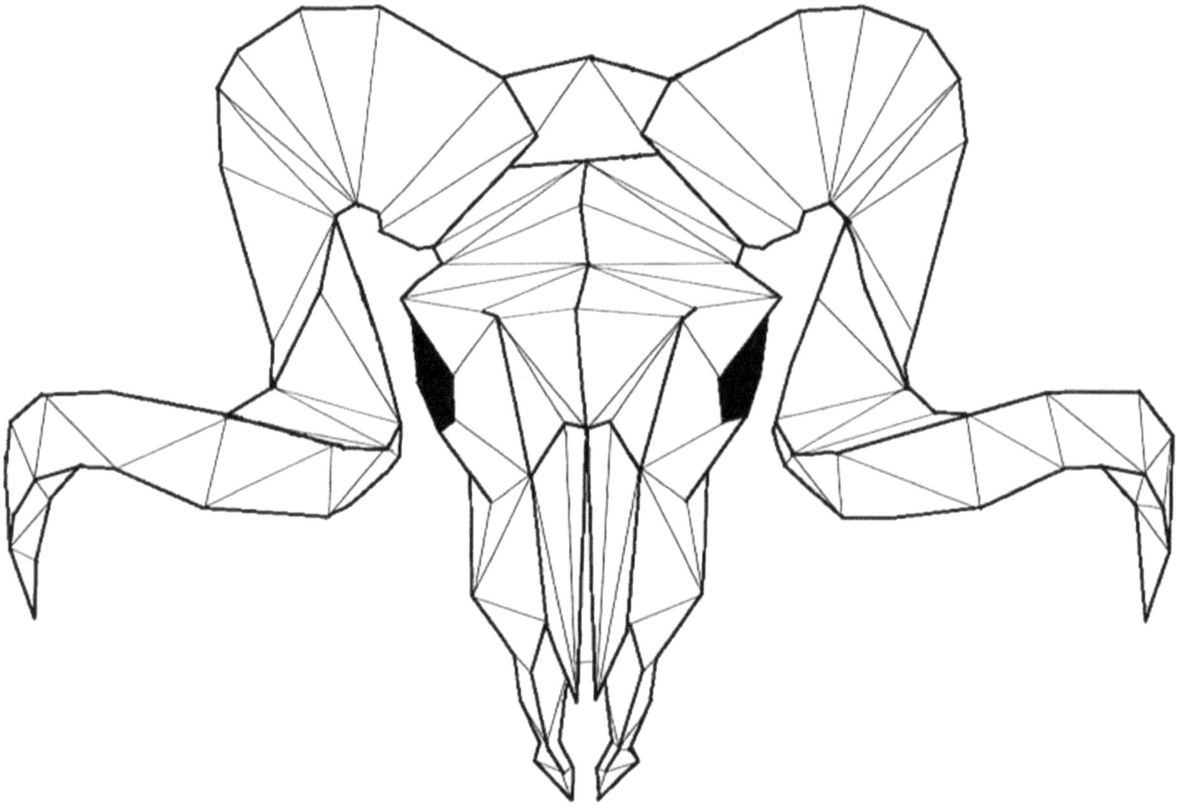

Copyrighted Material

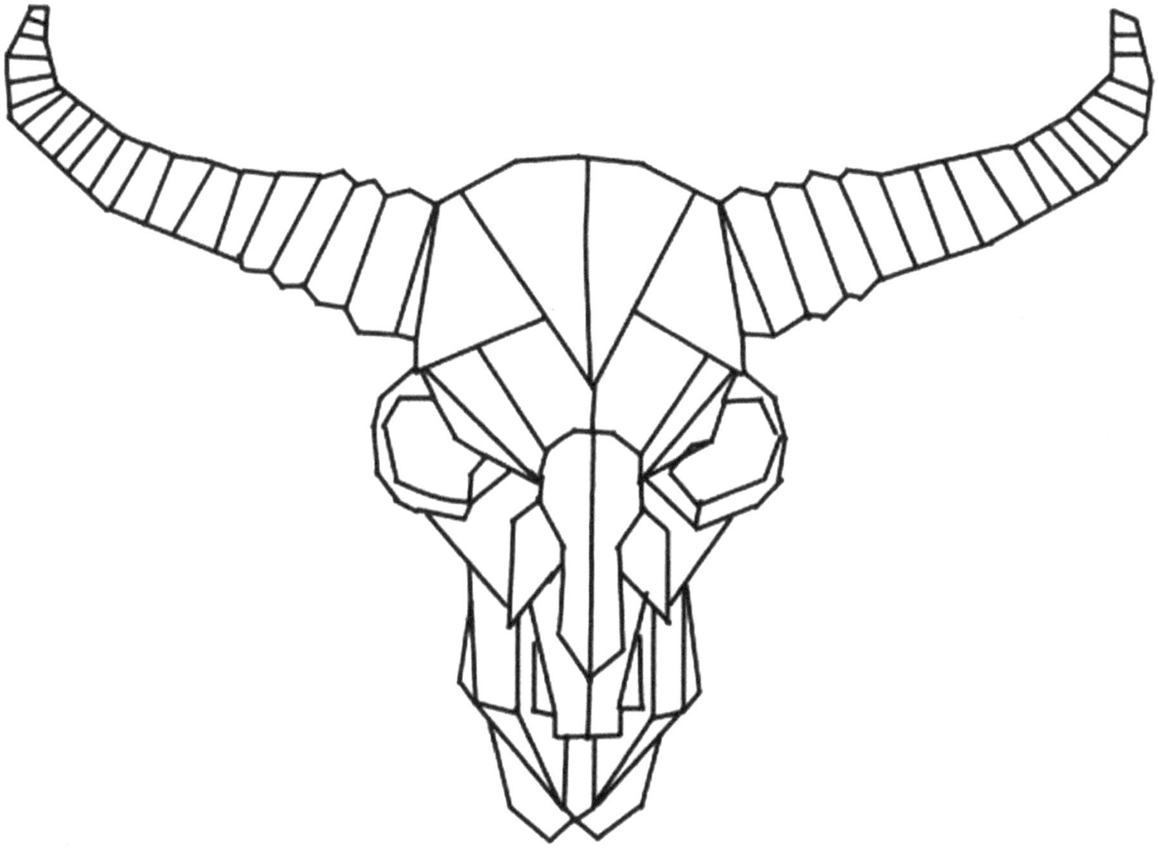

Copyrighted Material

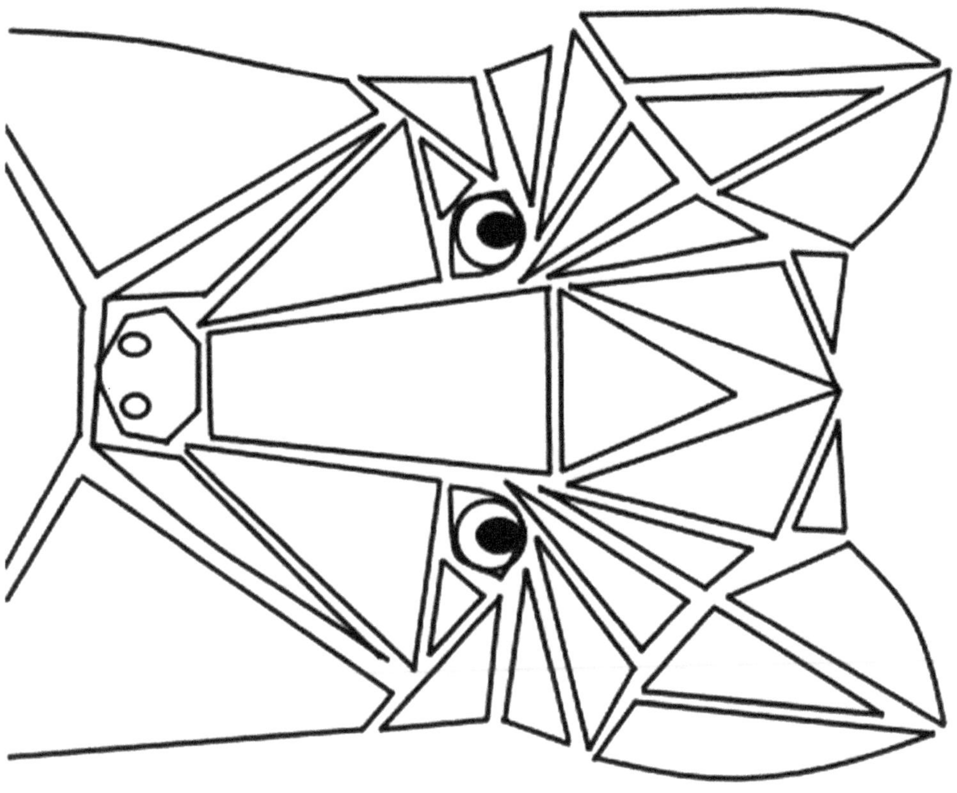

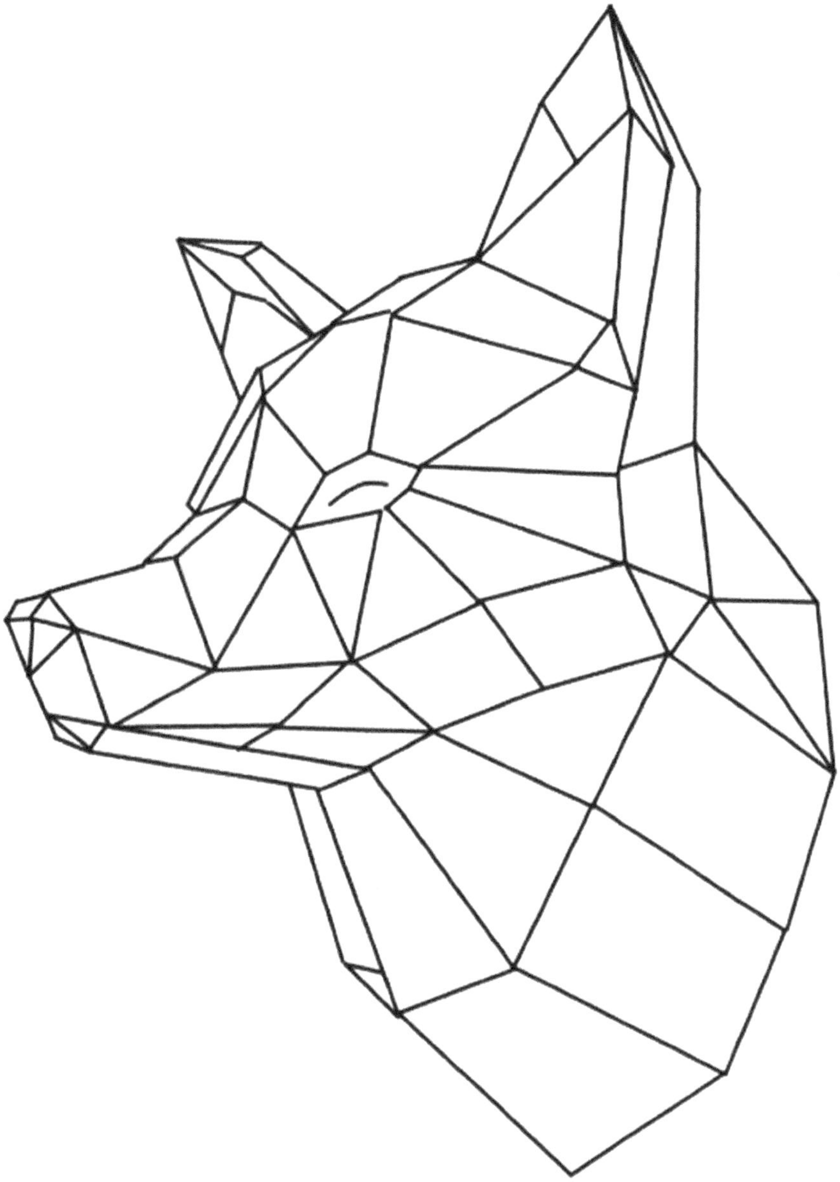

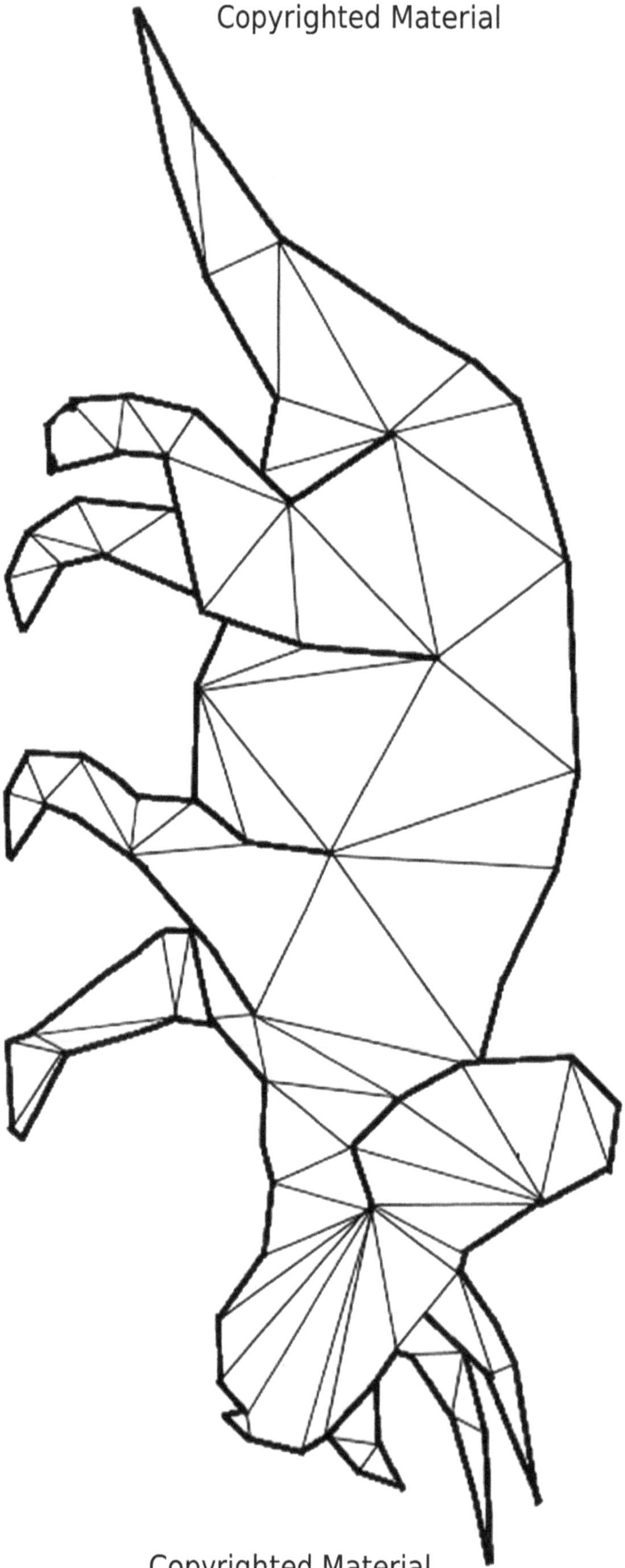

Copyrighted Material

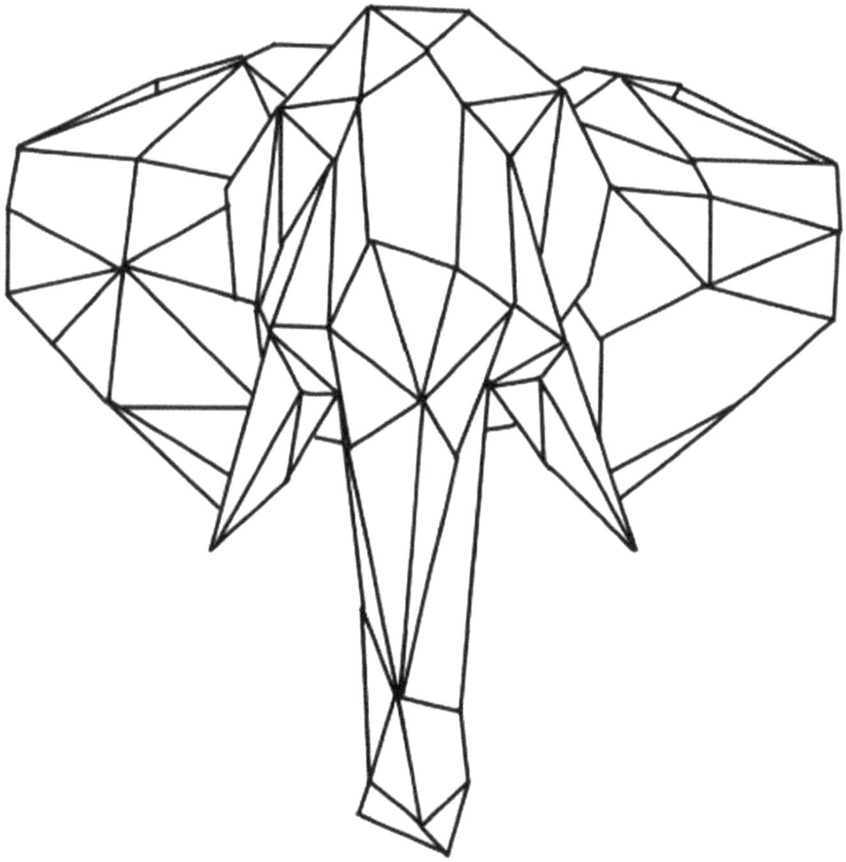

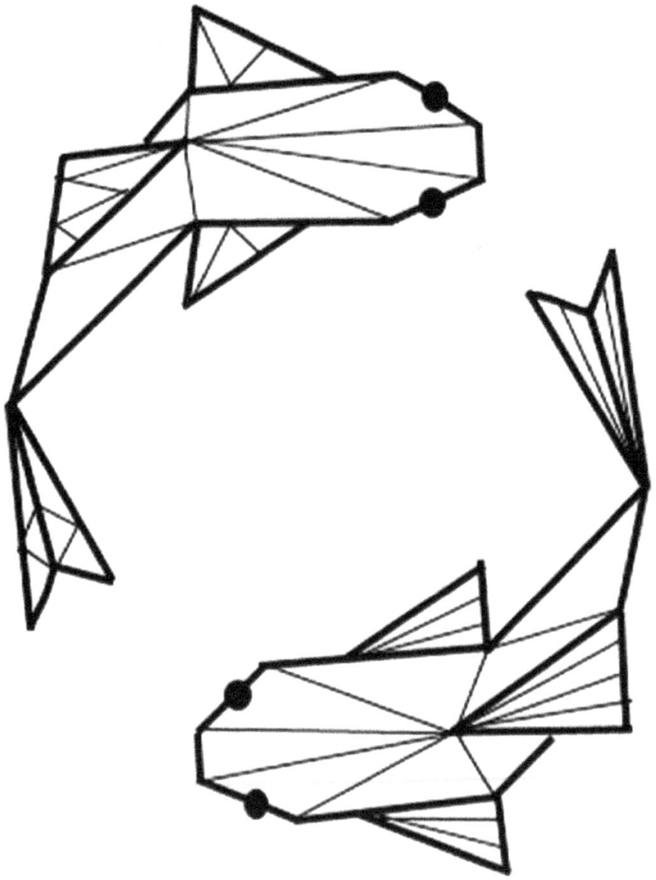

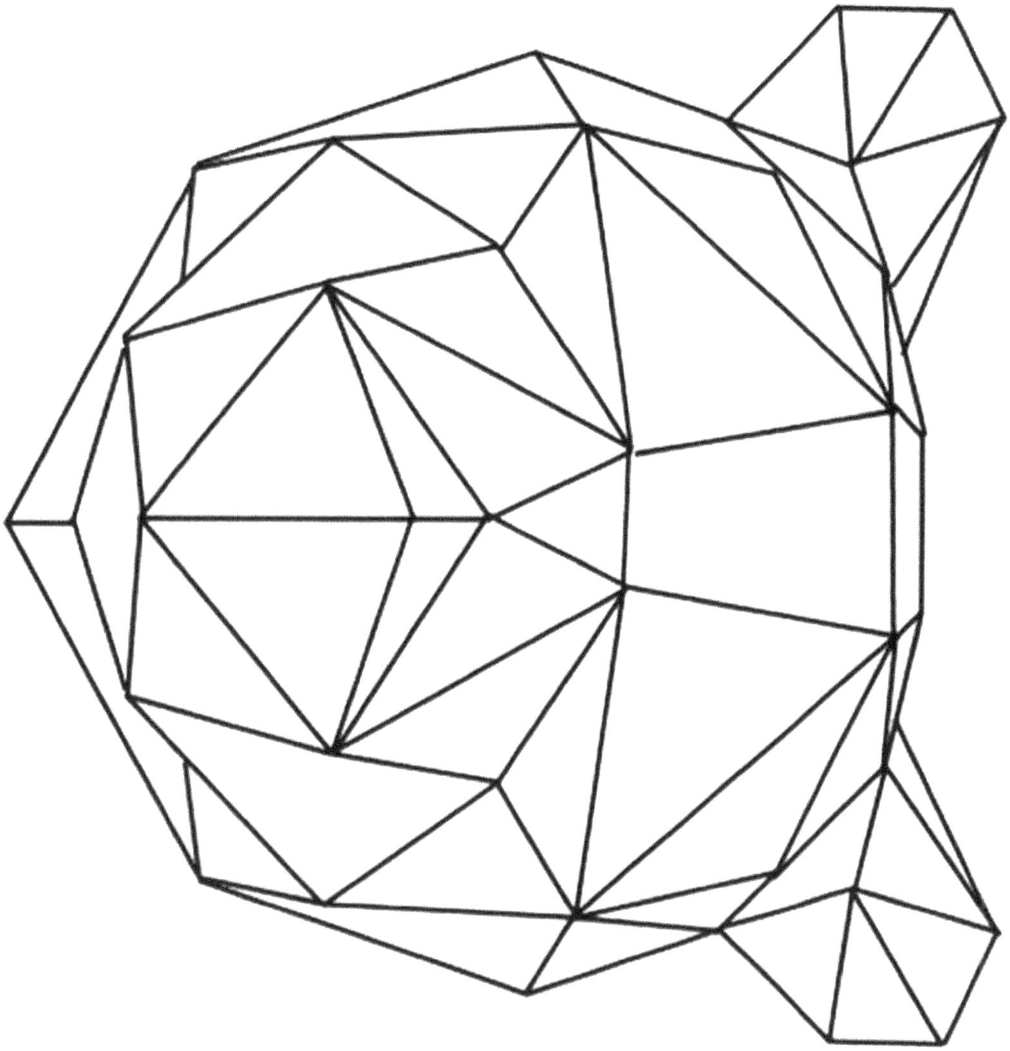

Copyrighted Material

www.ingramcontent.com/pod-product-compliance
Lightning Source LLC
Chambersburg PA
CBHW051839210526
45473CB00005B/1948
9781979991100